Us And Them

A Play

David Campton

Samuel French - London
New York - Toronto - Hollywood

© 1977 BY DAVID CAMPTON

Rights of Performance by Amateurs are controlled by Samuel French Ltd, 52 Fitzroy Street, London W1P 6JR, and they, or their authorized agents, issue licences to amateurs on payment of a fee. **It is an infringement of the Copyright to give any performance or public reading of the play before the fee has been paid and the licence issued.**

The Royalty Fee indicated below is subject to contract and subject to variation at the sole discretion of Samuel French Ltd.

> Basic fee for each and every
> performance by amateurs   Code D
> in the British Isles

The publication of this play does not imply that it is necessarily available for performance by amateurs or professionals, either in the British Isles or Overseas. Amateurs and professionals considering a production are strongly advised in their own interests to apply to the appropriate agents for consent before starting rehearsals or booking a theatre or hall.

ESSEX COUNTY LIBRARIES

ISBN 0 573 02346 8

Please see page iv for further copyright information.

CHARACTERS

Recorder
Spokesman A
Spokesman B
Other As
Other Bs

COPYRIGHT INFORMATION

(See also page ii)

This play is fully protected under the Copyright Laws of the British Commonwealth of Nations, the United States of America and all countries of the Berne and Universal Copyright Conventions.

All rights, including Stage, Motion Picture, Radio, Television, Public Reading, and Translation into Foreign Languages, are strictly reserved.

No part of this publication may lawfully be reproduced in ANY form or by any means—photocopying, typescript, recording (including video-recording), manuscript, electronic, mechanical, or otherwise—or be transmitted or stored in a retrieval system, without prior permission.

Licences for amateur performances are issued subject to the understanding that it shall be made clear in all advertising matter that the audience will witness an amateur performance; that the names of the authors of the plays shall be included on all announcements and on all programmes; and that the integrity of the authors' work will be preserved.

The Royalty Fee is subject to contract and subject to variation at the sole discretion of Samuel French Ltd.

In Theatres or Halls seating Six Hundred or more the fee will be subject to negotiation.

In Territories Overseas the fee quoted in this Acting Edition may not apply. A fee will be quoted on application to our local authorized agent, or if there is no such agent, on application to Samuel French Ltd, London.

VIDEO RECORDING OF AMATEUR PRODUCTIONS

Please note that the copyright laws governing video-recording are extremely complex and that it should not be assumed that any play may be video-recorded *for whatever purpose* without first obtaining the permission of the appropriate agents. The fact that a play is published by Samuel French Ltd does not indicate that video rights are available or that Samuel French Ltd controls such rights.

PRODUCTION NOTE

This play was written to be performed by a company of almost any size, of any age, and of either sex. The number against a character (A1, B2) is intended to indicate who makes a statement, asks a question, replies, or interjects, but the dialogue should be shared among the whole company. That is to say, although an A1 character should not speak B2 lines, there can be any number of A1 characters.

However, because the lines have been shorn of characterizing devices, the characters should not be treated as featureless machines. They are people. Character should be projected on to the lines (which is a reversal of the usual process).

The effect to aim at is of one conversation, emphasizing the fact that there is no difference between the people on either side of the wall. They are really part of one group.

US AND THEM

A bare stage. The Recorder enters with a large book and pen. He looks around

Recorder How odd. I felt sure there was someone here. Just a minute ago. There's still the trace of an echo. I could have been mistaken, though. They come and go.... Well, it's my job to wait and see. (*He makes himself comfortable*) I may have to wait some time.... But there's nothing I can do about that. Time passes. (*Pause*) Listen. Footsteps coming from this direction. And more footsteps coming from that direction. Something is about to happen. I must make a note.

Parties A and B enter from opposite sides. They pause wearily

"Party A from the East. Party B from the West. Worn out with travelling they come to rest." (*He ponders over the last note*) Verse in an official record? (*He crosses out the last words*) "At first they are too exhausted for words." . . . That's better. "Gradually they look around them, at first critically, then with growing admiration and delight. But too taken with their own concerns to notice the other group."

A1 Here?
B1 Here.
A1 It's a good place.
B1 Yes, it's a good place.
A2 Better than any other place we've seen.
B2 It's a good place all right.
A1 To pause at.
B1 To stay at.
A2 To make our own.
B2 For ever and ever.
A1 This is our place.
B1 Ours.

A2 Ours.
B2 We took long enough to find it.
A3 It was a long journey.
B3 But it was worth every day we searched.
A1 It was worth every mile we tramped.
B1 Look at it.
A2 Just look.
B2 Look here.
A3 Look there.
B3 Look.
A1 Look.

They point out things that please them

Recorder Of course, they could have commented on the natural advantages of the place—such as the average hours of sunshine, the mean rainfall, the geological structure, the chemistry of the topsoil, and the lush pasturage. They'll find the words in time. But next they notice each other.

From pointing out the delights of the place, the parties point to each other

A1 Look.
B1 Look.
A2 Look!
B2 Look!!

The groups chatter excitedly among themselves

Recorder Party A goes into a huddle, looking warily at Party B. Party B goes into a huddle, looking warily at Party A. Nothing to comment on there. It's the usual pattern. Any minute now the Spokesmen will face up to each other.

A Spokesman from Party B steps forward

Spokesman B Who are you?

A Spokesman from Party A steps forward

Spokesman A Who are *you*?
Spokesman B We've come a long way.
Spokesman A *We've* come a long way.

The Spokesmen return to their groups for quick conferences. After a few seconds they face each other again

Spokesman A We want to live here.
Spokesman B *We* want to live here.

The Spokesmen return to their groups for quick conferences. After a few seconds they face each other again

Spokesman B We won't let you drive us away.
Spokesman A We don't want to drive you away.

The Spokesmen return to their groups for conferences

Recorder One man, one vote. It takes time, but that's Democracy. There's no guarantee that they'll come to the right decision in the end, but that's Democracy, too. Not that I'm complaining about Democracy. It encourages a sense of responsibility. In theory, anyway.

The Spokesmen turn and face each other

Spokesman A Isn't there enough room for all of us?
Spokesman B There's enough room for everybody.
Spokesman A You could have all you see from there to here.
Spokesman B You could have all you see from here to there.
Spokesman A Agreed?
Spokesman B Agreed.

The As and Bs shout "Agreed". The Spokesmen shake hands

Spokesman A Do you mind if we pause in negotiations?
Spokesman B For a conference?
Spokesman A Agreed.

They go into conference again

Recorder Proposals, counter-proposals, resolutions, amendments, points of order, appeals to the chair, motions, votes, polls, divisions, objections, and recounts. Everybody has a say. It can become tedious, but it has one advantage—if anything goes wrong, everyone is to blame.

Spokesman A We have come to a conclusion.
Spokesman B A conclusion is a good thing to come to. We have reached an agreement.

Spokesman A It's always as well to reach an agreement.
Spokesman B That you take that stretch of country with all its natural amenities, grazing rights, water rights, hunting rights, fishing rights, arable land, and mineral deposits.
Spokesman A And that you take that stretch of land with all its natural amenities, etcetera, etcetera, etcetera.
Spokesman B Furthermore...
Spokesman A Furthermore?
Spokesman B Yes, furthermore. For the benefit of all concerned...
Spokesman A Does that include us?
Spokesman B It includes everybody. That a line be drawn.
Recorder (*musing aloud*) A line?
Spokesman B A line. That a line be drawn to mark the place where your land ends and ours begins.
Spokesman A Ah, yes. I was just about to add that a line be drawn to mark the place where our land ends and yours begins.
Spokesman B Good fences make good neighbours.
Spokesman A Good neighbours make good fences.
Spokesman B Shall we mark it now?
Spokesman A Why not?
Spokesman B Chalk?
Spokesman A String.

Spokesman A produces a length of string and the two groups join forces in surveying the ground, and pegging out the string in a straight line. Everyone has his own idea how the job should be done, but eventually it is finished

Recorder I don't know who gave me this job. I seem to have been doing it as long as I can remember. Not that I'm complaining—someone has to do it. The record has to be kept. Who knows—one day someone may learn from it.

The groups stand back and admire their handiwork

Spokesman A It's a good line.
Spokesman B Though I say it myself.
A1 I don't know.
Spokesman A Are you criticizing this line?
Spokesman B Perhaps you could make a better line.

Us and Them

Spokesman A We're all listening. What have you got against this line?

A1 Chickens.

As and Bs Chickens? What have chickens got to do with it? Take no notice. Got chickens on the brain.

A1 I know something about chickens, I do. There's not much you can tell me about chickens. I was brought up with chickens. And I'll tell you this: chickens can't read.

Spokesman B Chickens can't read?

Spokesman A What difference does that make to this line?

A1 None at all to your line.

Spokesman B Or to your chickens for that matter.

A1 No use putting up your "Beware of the Bull" signs. No use sticking up your "Trespassers will be Prosecuted" notices. And you might as well forget your "One-Way Streets", your "Diversions", and your "Roads Closed". The chickens go where they want to go. No use drawing a line, and expecting the chickens to stay on this side of it. Or on that side of it for that matter.

As and Bs True. That's a point. I never saw a chicken reading. Or taking any notice of a line.

Spokesman B But what does it matter where the chickens go?

A1 Oh, if it doesn't matter there's no more to be said.

Spokesman A Good. Now we can get on with . . .

A2 But suppose it should be sheep.

B1 Sheep?

A2 Sheep can't read either. At least I never saw a sheep reading. Ignorant animals really.

B1 A line won't keep a sheep from straying.

B2 Especially if they can't read.

A3 Or cows from wandering.

B3 Or horses from getting lost.

A2 And as for rabbits . . .

Spokesman B All right. What do you want?

Spokesman A Schools for animals?

A1 What we need are fences.

B1 Walls.

A2 Thick enough to stop cows from breaking through.

B2 High enough to stop chickens from flying over.

A3 Good walls make good neighbours.

B3 Good neighbours make good walls.
Spokesman A You want walls?
Spokesman B Shall we build walls?
A1 Before we do anything else.

Spokesman A and Spokesman B take opposite ends of the piece of string, and raise it about six inches off the ground

Spokesman A This high?
B1 Higher. Think of the cows.

The string is raised waist high

Spokesman B This high?
A2 Higher. Think of the horses.

The string is raised shoulder high

Spokesman A This high?
B2 Higher. Think of the chickens.

The string is held as high as the Spokesmen can reach, standing on tiptoe

Spokesman B I think that should do.
B1 Yes, that should do.
Spokesman A It had better do. Now make it fast.

The ends of the string are tied to posts

Spokesman B And build the wall.

The wall is built. This can be done in a number of ways. Blocks could be built up to the height of the string, or more string could be tied between the posts, or material could be draped over the string. At all events it is achieved after a great deal of activity. Meanwhile, the Recorder looks on, and takes notes

Recorder I won't say they're right. I won't say they're wrong. It's my job merely to record events. Events speak for themselves. They wanted a wall: they've got a wall. Neither side can see over, or through, or round. That's a wall.

Now all the As are on one side of the wall, and all the Bs are on the other side

Spokesman A That's a wall. That ought to last.

Us and Them

Spokesman B Nothing we need to learn about making a wall.
Recorder Except how to make a way over, or through, or round.
Spokesman A Are you there?
Spokesman B We're here. Are you all satisfied?
Spokesman A Everything went according to plan. What now?
Spokesman B We settle down. And you?
Spokesman A We settle down, too. It's good land.
Spokesman B It's very good land. We're lucky. We've got good neighbours.
Spokesman A We've got good neighbours, too. It's a good wall.
Spokesman B Good walls make good neighbours.
Spokesman A Good neighbours make good walls.
Spokesman B Good-bye, then. There's work to be done.
Spokesman A Good-bye. Must get down to work.

Shouting "Good-bye" the two groups pick up their belongings, and move away. The "Good-byes" die away in the distance

Recorder Nothing left but the wall. And the chickens on each side of the wall. And the sheep on each side of the wall. And the cows on each side of the wall. And the horses on each side of the wall. And the people on each side of the wall . . .

The groups re-appear on each side of the wall. They are all working

It's a busy life—and the great advantage with being busy is that it occupies the mind. Working keeps thoughts under control. Thoughts are more apt to run wild than any sheep. Thoughts can fly higher than any chickens. In fact walls make thoughts fly even higher. But as long as thoughts are kept under control there's no harm done. Except that there comes a time when all the chickens have been fed; all the cows have been milked; all the sheep have been rounded up in the fold—and thoughts are free to stray.

Gradually the groups give up work, and make themselves comfortable

A1 I wonder what they're doing over there.
A2 Over there?

B1 Over there. What do you think they're doing?
A2 Why?
A1 Why not?
A2 Why do you wonder what they're doing over there?
B1 We can't see them, can we?
B2 They can't see us.
A1 I just wondered.
B1 Anybody can wonder.
A1 Just a thought—like do spring and summer come before autumn and winter, or do autumn and winter come first?
B1 Like—can a worm think?
A1 Like—what are they doing over there?
A2 The usual things, I suppose.
B2 They'll be doing the usual things.
A1 What do you mean—the usual things?
A2 Things that you usually do.
B2 Things that we usually do.
B1 Not the things that *they* usually do?
A2 The things that they usually do.
B1 You said the things that *we* usually do.
A2 They're the same things.
B1 Are they the same?
A2 Why shouldn't they be the same?
B2 Why should they be the same?
A1 They're not like us.
A2 Aren't they?
B1 It stands to reason.
A1 Work it out for yourself.
B1 Just work it out.
A1 For instance—you're not like me, are you?
A2 Not much.
B1 You're not a bit like me.
A2 So they're not like us.
B2 So they're not a bit like us.
A2 We're on this side of the wall.
B2 They're on the other side of the wall.
A1 Fancy living on the other side of the wall.
B1 Fancy wanting to live on the other side of the wall.
A2 When you could be living here.
B2 Fancy not wanting to live here.

Us and Them

A1 Funny.
B1 They've got some funny ways.
A1 Yes, they've got some funny ways.
B2 Have they?
A2 Of course. You've got some funny ways, too.
B1 They look funny to me all right.
A2 We've all got funny ways.
B2 But their ways are funnier. Over there.
B1 We don't even know what ways they've got.
A2 If they've got ways we don't know about, they must be funny ways.
A1 Still, as long as they're on the other side of the wall, it doesn't matter.
B1 It doesn't matter as long as they're on that side, and we're on this.
A2 I'm not so sure.
A1 What do you mean?
B1 I've been thinking. They're very quiet.
B2 We're quiet.
B1 We've got nothing to make a noise about.
A2 What about them, eh?
A1 What about them?
A2 What have they got to be so quiet about?
B1 It's unnatural.
A1 It's unusual.
B2 It's disturbing.
A2 It's disquieting.
B1 It's abnormal.
A1 It's uncomfortable.
B2 It's sinister.
A2 It's not as it should be.
B1 It's enough to send cold shivers down your back.
A1 It's enough to make your hair stand on end.
B2 Just thinking about it.
A2 Just wondering.
B1 What are they up to?
A2 What are they doing behind that wall?
B2 They could be doing anything behind that wall.
B1 Like what?
A2 Just think.

B1 Ah!
B2 Oh!
A1 They wouldn't.
B2 Not that!
A2 I wouldn't put it past 'em.
B2 Not them!
A1 Not that!
A2 Not what?
A1 Not what you're thinking.
B2 Oh, would they really?
B1 They're not to be relied on.
A1 You're exaggerating.
A2 Exaggerating?
A1 You wouldn't expect anybody to do that.
B2 We wouldn't do it.
B1 We're not like them.
A2 They're not like us.
B2 But they wouldn't. Not . . .
B1 Like . . .
A2 For instance . . .
B1 Or even . . .
A1 Not to mention . . .
A2 Just you wait.
A1 Wait for what?
B1 You'll see. You'll believe me then.
A2 Just you wait till you see it happening.
B2 I don't believe it.
A1 Oh!
A2 You will.
B1 If you ask me, they're wicked.
B2 Stands to reason. They're a wicked lot.
A1 They wouldn't get up to that sort of thing if they weren't wicked.
A2 Well, as long as they're wicked on their side of the wall . . .
A1 Wickedness spreads.
B1 Wickedness creeps.
A2 How long will they go on being wicked on their side of the wall?
B2 It's a high wall.
A1 It's a thick wall.

Us and Them

B3 Let them do what they like on their side of the wall.
A3 They can't interfere with us.
A1 Can't they?
B1 What can they do to us?
A2 They could be making plans now.
B2 Think. Just think.
A1 They could be spying on us now.
B3 Don't be silly.
A3 That's absurd.
A1 Is it?
B1 Perhaps we ought to check.
A2 It wouldn't do any harm to look.
A3 You can look if you like.
B3 I'm not making a fool of myself.
A3 I'll tell you what they're doing on the other side.
A2 What?
B3 I know what they're doing.
B2 Tell us.
A3 They're lying down in the sun like sensible people, maybe chewing long bits of grass.
B3 They're looking up at the sky, and working out tomorrow's weather.
A3 Or they're counting chickens.
B3 Or counting sheep.
A3 They're doing what we're doing.
B3 They're doing exactly what we're doing.
A1 I knew they weren't to be trusted.
B1 Have a look quickly.
A2 Look at them.
B2 Look.
A1 Look.
B1 How?
A2 Climb up.
B2 Look over the top.

They prepare to climb the wall with whatever means are at hand—blocks, furniture, or each other

Recorder At this point there is always the temptation to shout "stop". But a Recorder mustn't. It's a Recorder's job to record: no more, no less. And, my goodness the fuss that's made about handwriting and spelling! As if spelling mattered after ... they've taken the first steps, you see. And after the first steps the others follow naturally. All a Recorder can do is to record. They climb to the top of the wall, and ...

The As, who have now reached the top of the wall, come face to face with the Bs. They all shriek, and clamber down again

A1 It's all true.
B1 They were.
A1 Looking over.
B1 Spying.
A1 On us.
B1 On us.
A1 It's a good job we looked.
B1 We caught them at it.
A1 And were they surprised!
B1 They never expected that.
A1 They were fairly caught.
B1 Caught in the act.
A2 But why were they doing it?
B2 Why would they want to do it?
A2 Why?
B2 Why?
A1 Ah-ha.
B1 We can guess.
A1 That's only half the story.
B1 That's only the tip of the iceberg.
A1 They're up to no good.
B1 They're ready for something.
A1 We must be ready for them.
B2 Ready for what?
A1 Ready for anything.
B1 Anything might happen.
A1 They're not like us.
B1 They're a bad lot.
A1 They're cruel.
B1 They're ruthless.
A1 Devilish.
B1 Fiendish.
A1 Wild.

Us and Them

B1 Savages.
A1 Peeping Toms.
B1 Sneaks.
A3 But let's consider.
B3 Let's think carefully.
A3 We looked over the wall, too.
B3 We'd never have seen them if we hadn't peeped.
A1 It's as well that we did.
B1 Where should we be now if we hadn't?
A3 Wait, though. Couldn't we forget that it happened?
B3 Couldn't we make allowances?
A1 Oh, yes, indeed.
B1 Why not, indeed?
A1 If we *want* to be made into mince.
B1 If we want to wake up with our throats cut.
A2 But what can we do?
B2 What's to be done?
A1 One thing's certain.
B1 There's no doubt at all.
A1 We can't live here any longer with them just there.
B1 We'll either have to fight or move on.
A1 Either they go, or we'll have to go.
B1 It's them or us.
As and Bs Them.
A3 But we've got the wall.
B3 There's always the wall.
As and Bs Pull it down. Pull it down.

Both sides attack the wall

Recorder It's odd: even sensible actions that would never be taken in the cause of peace are taken in the name of war. Like all pulling together. Like breaking down walls. But the result isn't the same. As for instance . . .

The wall falls. For a second the two sides stare at each other. Then, with a cry, they rush at each other. They fight

Some are forced off-stage. Some run off-stage and are pursued. Some fall and are dragged away by friends

They fight. No, I'm not recording all the details. Any battle is just like any other battle. There are some acts of chivalry, some deeds of treachery, a hint of courage, a touch of cowardice. But the heroes, and the cowards, and the patriots, and the traitors have one thing in common: they all end up as dead as each other. This is nothing. I've seen battles that make this look like a squabble between sticklebacks. Not that I'm offering any prizes for the best battle. Every battle ends in the same way. One side thinks it has won; the other side thinks it ought to have won. Someone cleans up the mess, and the ground is left clean and tidy—ready for someone else to fight over another time. I could moralize. I could draw conclusions. But the conclusion is so obvious. The facts speak for themselves. They fight until . . . Oh, is it over already?

The stage is clear

Now, is there anything to add before I draw the line? No? I had a feeling that there might be. Like the last spark in a dying fire. Like the last syllable of a fading echo. Ah, I thought as much.

An A and a B limp on to the stage from opposite sides. They come face to face where the wall once stood

A Going?
B Going.
A You could stay—now.
B No, we can't stay—now.
A It's good land.
B It was good land.
A We—we didn't want to—to . . .
B If only we hadn't . . .
A But you . . .
B We?
A We, too.
B It was the wall, you know.
A The wall was to blame.
B The wall.
A The wall.
B We should have made it stronger.
A Thicker.

B Higher.
A Longer.
B It was the wall.

They go out on opposite sides

The Recorder slams the book shut, and jumps up angrily

Recorder I don't want to know any more. It's all down here. Over and over again. History. The record is kept because someday someone may learn from it. Now I'm required elsewhere. Oh, this all becomes so monotonous. (*He starts to walk away, but pauses*) Someday. Somewhere. Someone. Is it possible? Hah!

He goes

Black-out

MADE AND PRINTED IN GREAT BRITAIN BY
LATIMER TREND & COMPANY LTD PLYMOUTH
MADE IN ENGLAND